MW00736724

About the Artist

Angelea Van Dam of Hello Angel has drawn her entire life. This New Zealand artist is a graphic designer by trade, working out of her home as a freelancer. Her color style is every color under the sun and then she likes to pile on some more! Angelea wants to be in her studio making art almost all the time. It's what makes her happy. The fact that her art inspires others makes her doubly happy and motivates her to create so much more.

Color Your World with Hello Angel Coloring

ISBN 978-1-64178-007-0

Fox Chapel Publishing makes every effort to use environmentally friendly paper for printing.

© 2018 by Hello Angel/Artlicensing.com and Quiet Fox Designs, *www.QuietFoxDesigns.com*, an imprint of Fox Chapel Publishing, 800-457-9112, 903 Square Street, Mount Joy, PA 17552.

We are always looking for talented authors. To submit an idea, please send a brief inquiry to acquisitions@foxchapelpublishing.com.

Printed in China
First printing